UNLOCKING LIFE'S SECRETS

26 LESSONS FOR EXTRAORDINARY SUCCESS

Manan Verma & Belle Yip

PAPER2PUBISH
www.paper2publish.com
India || USA || Russia || Nigeria || Singapore

Published By:
PAPER2PUBLISH
India || USA || Russia || Nigeria || Singapore

Unlocking Life's Secrets
By: Manan Verma & Belle Yip

Published by:
Paper2Publish
India, Uttarakhand,249407
www.paper2publish.com

ISBN: 978-93-6029-989-7

Editor: Sneha Mehra

Dedicated to you the believer It's time you start believing in the power within you.

Introduction

Success is not merely a destination; it is a transformative journey filled with challenges, growth, and the realization of potential. At the heart of this journey lies the crucial first step: **Action**. Taking proactive steps toward your goals is the cornerstone of all achievement. Without action, dreams remain distant aspirations, elusive and unattainable. The moment you decide to take that first step, you break free from inertia, opening yourself to possibilities you might never have imagined. Action creates momentum, enabling you to progress toward your goals. Every small decision to act—whether taking on a new project, learning a new skill, or reaching out to someone for guidance—cumulatively shapes your future. The journey of a thousand miles truly begins with that single, courageous step.

As you embark on this path, the importance of **Belief** and **Courage** cannot be overstated. Cultivating a strong belief in yourself is essential; it is the unwavering faith that fuels your ambitions and allows you to rise above doubt. When you believe in yourself, you arm yourself with the confidence to face obstacles head-on. Challenges are inevitable in any journey, but it is courage that allows you to confront them. Courage is not the absence of fear; rather, it is the willingness to push through that fear in pursuit of your goals. Together, belief and courage create a powerful synergy that not only strengthens your resolve but also propels you forward in the face of adversity. They lay the groundwork for resilience and determination, equipping you with the mindset needed to navigate life's uncertainties.

A pivotal aspect of your journey is the understanding of **Destiny**. Destiny is not a predetermined path; it is the result of the choices and actions you take every day. When you recognize that your actions shape your destiny, you empower yourself to take control of your future. Each decision, each moment of action, contributes to the story of your life. You transition from being a passive participant in your fate to an active creator of your destiny. This perspective inspires a sense of ownership over your journey and encourages you to make intentional choices that align with your aspirations. The realization that you have the power to influence your destiny can be a profound motivator, propelling you to seize opportunities and overcome obstacles.

As you move forward, **Effort** and **Focus** become indispensable elements of your success. Giving your best in every endeavor is essential; it signifies commitment and determination. It is not enough to take action; you must also pour your heart into that action, ensuring that it aligns with your values and aspirations. Equally important is the need for focus. In our fast-paced world, distractions abound, and maintaining focus can be challenging. However, staying concentrated on your goals enables you to channel your energy effectively, minimizing waste and maximizing impact. When effort is combined with focus, you create a powerful force that drives progress and propels you toward success.

Your journey is also marked by the themes of **Growth** and **Learning**. Every experience, whether positive or negative, holds valuable lessons. Embracing these experiences as opportunities for growth is vital. It is through facing challenges that we learn resilience, adaptability, and resourcefulness. Each setback presents a chance to reflect, reassess, and ultimately grow stronger. This commitment to growth allows you to evolve, honing your skills and expanding your perspective. Moreover, the journey itself is as important as the destination. Embracing every step, every twist and turn, equips you with wisdom and insights that enrich your experience and shape your character.

Hope and **Inspiration** are essential elements that keep the flame of possibility alive. Hope acts as a guiding light, illuminating the path ahead even in the darkest of times. It instills a sense of optimism and encourages you to believe that better days are possible. Alongside hope, inspiration plays a crucial role in fueling your journey. It can come from various sources—books, mentors, or the achievements of others. It ignites your passion and reminds you of the greatness that lies within you. When hope and inspiration intertwine, they create a potent force that propels you forward, motivating you to pursue your dreams with unwavering determination.

The journey is also about recognizing **Opportunities** and embracing your **Passions**. Life presents countless opportunities for growth and advancement; it is up to you to recognize and seize them. Each opportunity serves as a stepping stone toward your aspirations, and pursuing your passions adds meaning to your journey. When you engage in activities that ignite your passion, you tap into your intrinsic motivation, making the journey more enjoyable and fulfilling. This alignment of passion and purpose enhances your drive, ensuring that you remain committed to your goals.

In the face of challenges, **Resilience** and the mindset of **Never-give-up** are essential for sustaining progress. Life will undoubtedly throw obstacles in your path, but it is your resilience that will determine how you respond. Resilience is the ability to bounce back from setbacks and adapt to changing circumstances. Cultivating this trait enables you to face adversity with grace and strength. Coupled with a never-give-up attitude, resilience ensures that you stay the course even when the going gets tough. This combination fosters persistence, allowing you to push through difficulties and emerge stronger on the other side.

By understanding these principles and integrating them into your daily life, you set the stage for your success. Remember, the journey is not a straight line but a series of twists, turns, and opportunities for growth. Your journey will be uniquely yours, shaped by your actions, beliefs, and the courage you summon along the way. As you navigate this path, embrace the lessons learned from each experience, recognize the importance of kindness and leadership, and strive for excellence in all that you do. Let your yearning for success and zeal for life drive you forward, and may this book serve as a guide to illuminate your way as you embark on your own remarkable journey toward achieving your dreams.

TOC

A Action: Taking Steps Toward Your Ambitions

B Believe: Believing In Yourself

C Courage: Challenges Without Fear

D Destiny: The Path You Create

E Effort: Giving Your Best

F Focus: Directing Your Energy

G Growth: Embracing Change and Learning

H Hope: The Light That Guides You

I Inspiration: The Spark That Ignites You

J Judgment: Making Wise Choices

K Knowledge: The Power of Understanding

L Leadership: Guiding and Inspiring Others

M Motivation: The Force That Drives You

N Never Give Up: Persistence in the Face of Challenges

O Opportunities: Recognizing and Seizing the Moment

P Passion: Fueling Your Purpose

Q Question: Seeking Knowledge and Understanding

R Resilience: Bouncing Back from Setbacks

S Success: Achieving Your Goals

T Teamwork: Collaboration and Synergy

U Unwavering: Staying True to Your Values

V Vision: Seeing the Bigger Picture

W Wisdom: Making Wise Decisions

X Excellence: Striving to Be Your Best
Y Yearning: The Desire for Growth and Fulfillment
Z Zeal: Enthusiasm and Passion for Life

A

Action

Taking Steps Toward Your Ambitions

Ambition, as an asset, acts as a catalyst for advancement, allowing us to aspire to achieve amazing accomplishments. However, ambition alone isn't adequate. Attaining aspirations demands active attention, an adaptable attitude, and absolute action. Ambition, although admirable, always asks for action aligned with awareness, otherwise it will remain abstract and aimless. Aspiring individuals who act, adjust, and adapt accelerate their ascent, attaining achievements that others admire.

The first action toward achieving any aspiration is acceptance. Accepting all aspects of who you are—your attributes, abilities, and areas for advancement—activates a sense of assurance. Without self-acceptance, ambition can feel awkward, almost alien, and the path will appear arduous. Yet, once you accept yourself, you allow your ambition to align with authenticity, which acts as an anchor to advance you. This acceptance creates an assurance that aids you as you apply action toward attaining your aims.

Achieving anything worthwhile demands active awareness and attention. You can't afford apathy or avoidance; instead, approach every aspect of your aspirations with absolute awareness. Awareness allows you to analyze what actions are advantageous and what adjustments are needed along the way. Agility is another asset you must adopt, as being adaptable in adverse situations accelerates your advancement. The ability to adjust with agility keeps you aligned with your ambition, even when adversity arises.

Ambition may be admirable, but achieving aspirations asks for arduous effort. You will encounter adversity and adjustments are always anticipated. You may have to abstain from activities that act as distractions. Allocating your attention and abilities toward achieving your aims often demands sacrifice. Abstaining from unnecessary associations or avoiding all avenues of amusement is part of ambition's ask. But if your ambition is aligned with your authentic self, these adjustments will appear as advantageous, acting as avenues for accelerated advancement.

Action must accompany ambition at all times. Without action, ambition is aimless, and without accountability, action is arbitrary. Accountability assures that each action aligns with your aspiration, accelerating your progress. Those who attain the apex of their ambition understand that active attention and accountability are always aligned. They approach adversity with agility, adjust their actions accordingly, and act consistently to advance toward their aims.

Now, think about this: only a small percentage of aspirants actually achieve the absolute apex of their ambitions. Why? Are they inherently advantaged? Not at all. What separates them is an active, adaptable attitude. They apply action to every area of ambition, adopting awareness and agility along the way. They aren't afraid to adjust their approach when adversity arises, and they remain accountable for their actions. Their advancement is assured because they act with absolute intention.

However, ambition alone isn't always advantageous. An essential aspect of ambition is adopting a balance. Advancement without awareness of your emotional well-being leads to an anxious, aimless existence. To achieve ambitions with happiness, you must allow a balance between aspiration and appreciation for the journey. Aligning your ambition with your authentic values will assure that you aren't abandoning happiness for hollow accomplishments.

In the end, advancement comes from adopting an active, adaptable approach, anchored by ambition. Always act with awareness, adjust with agility, and allow yourself to advance, all while appreciating the amazing adventure. Achieve your aims with absolute action, ambition, and an attitude that adapts to every adversity that comes your way.

B

Believe
Believing In Yourself

Believing in yourself is the backbone of every bold move you'll make in life. It's the bridge between where you are now and the breathtaking heights you want to reach. No matter the battles you face, believing in your potential can break down the barriers that stand in your way. The world will bring people who belittle your efforts, bash your dreams, or belabor your failures. There will be those who, instead of building you up, try to break you down, bruising your confidence along the way. But here's the beauty—your belief in yourself is stronger than any blow they can throw.

It all begins with the belief that you're capable of more. Every big achievement starts as a small, burning belief within that tells you, "Yes, I can." This belief blossoms into bravery, allowing you to take bold steps that others may be too afraid to attempt. But bravery isn't the absence of fear; it's the belief that you can face your fears and still move forward. Even if you stumble or fall, belief will bring you back to your feet, ready to try again.

Believing in yourself also builds resilience. When others try to bring you down, when the bumps in the road feel like barriers too big to break through, belief will be your beacon of light. It will help you bounce back from failures and setbacks, reminding you that no battle is too big if you truly believe in your ability to overcome it.

Don't let the beliefs of others bind you. There will always be people who criticize or cast doubt over your dreams. Some may claim to support you but bear false intentions, backing away when things get tough or betraying your trust behind your back. They may burden you with negativity, trying to blur your vision. But the truth is, you don't need anyone else to validate your vision or goals. Belief in yourself should be your biggest source of strength. It's the one thing no one can take from you, and it's the one thing that will bring you through every challenge, no matter how big or bad it seems.

Becoming the best version of yourself means trusting your own blueprint. You are building something unique, something beautiful, and that process requires boldness. Be brave enough to block out the noise, brave enough to make mistakes, and brave enough to try again. Every barrier can be broken if you have belief at your back.

Budding success starts with belief. It doesn't happen overnight, but the belief that it will happen, bit by bit, makes all the difference. Every journey begins with the belief that you are capable. By believing in your potential, you're not just opening doors—you're breaking them down.

So, keep believing in yourself, no matter what others may say. The brilliance of your belief will bring you to the brink of boundless possibilities. Don't back down when things feel bleak. Keep building on your belief every day, knowing it's the key to unlocking everything you've ever dreamed of.

Believe, and let that belief be your brightest beacon toward becoming everything you were meant to be. The journey is long, but belief will be the constant that carries you through every obstacle, bringing you ever closer to your dreams.

C

Courage
Challenges Without Fear

Courage is critical for confronting countless challenges. Consider this: in every corner of life, you need courage to cope with chaos, control crises, and cultivate confidence. Courage carries you through confusion, compels you to continue, and creates the capacity to conquer challenges, no matter how complex. Without courage, you may crumble under the pressure of criticism or complications, clinging to comfort instead of choosing change.

Courage is the catalyst for chasing your cherished dreams and carving out the course you crave. Challenges will come consistently, but courage will carry you through, even when circumstances seem cloudy or chaotic. Choosing courage is choosing to confront conflicts with composure, despite the constant current of uncertainty. It creates clarity when the road ahead seems cluttered with confusion, and it confirms your commitment to your calling.

Courageous people constantly challenge themselves to continue climbing toward their goals, even when conditions are complicated. They don't compromise their vision for the comfort of consensus. Instead, they cultivate courage, knowing it's the core component of success. They confront challenges with calm confidence, carrying on even when crowds are absent. A courageous person doesn't cling to the need for constant support or confirmation from others. They create their own confidence, continuing despite criticism or conflict. They chart their own course, confident that courage will carry them through any challenge.

When you consider your own life, courage should be the compass that directs your decisions. Countless choices will require courage—whether it's committing to change, confronting a conflict, or challenging yourself to climb higher. Courage is a crucial characteristic that compels you to continue even when conditions are confusing or complex.

It creates the confidence to cope with setbacks and carry on when success seems far off. Without courage, many will choose complacency, comfortable in their current circumstances, content with avoiding challenges.

Courageous individuals don't count on comfort or convenience. They consciously choose courage, even when confronted with criticism, chaos, or change. They commit to their course and cultivate the confidence to continue, even when the path is cluttered with complications. They don't collapse under the weight of criticism or challenge; instead, they confront these circumstances with calm, clear conviction, knowing that courage is the constant companion of those who chase greatness.

Courage also compels you to carry on without the certainty of success. You can't calculate every outcome or control every consequence, but you can commit to continue despite the complexities. Courageous people confront their fears and choose to continue, crafting their path with consistent effort. They don't wait for conditions to be perfect or for a crowd to cheer them on. They carry the confidence that courage will see them through, no matter how challenging the course becomes.

In conclusion, courage is central to claiming the life you want. It compels you to confront challenges, cultivate confidence, and continue climbing toward your dreams. When courage becomes your constant companion, you'll create the life you crave, regardless of the circumstances. Keep courage at the core of every choice, and you'll find that no challenge is too great to conquer.

D

Destiny
The Path You Create

Destiny is a dynamic force that directs our decisions and defines our destination. It plays a dominant role in determining the direction of our lives. While determination, discipline, and drive are decisive factors in our endeavours, destiny ultimately dictates the final destination. Destiny isn't just a distant force; it's a delicate dance between what we desire and what's destined to be.

Each day, every decision you make adds depth to the design of your destiny. Destiny demands dedication, a deep dive into who you are and what you want to do. You dedicate yourself to your dreams, drive yourself to achieve them, and devote countless hours to developing your skills. Yet, at the end of the day, destiny decides. It determines whether your efforts will deliver the desired outcome or whether it will direct you toward a different destination.

Destiny doesn't diminish the value of your dedication. Instead, it deepens it. It's a reminder that even in the most difficult moments, when you feel defeated or delayed, your destiny is still in development.

Sometimes, destiny delivers you to destinations that differ from your original design, but these deviations often lead to discoveries that define your path more clearly. Destiny allows for detours that can be delightful and, at times, demanding, but they are always part of the grander design.

When thinking about destiny, don't let doubt dominate. Destiny is not a discouraging force but a directive one. It drives you to dig deeper into yourself, to discover what you're truly devoted to, and to determine the direction that aligns with your deepest desires. Destiny encourages you to be daring and decisive, to dream bigger, and to develop a determination that is unwavering despite the detours and delays.

In this dynamic dance with destiny, adaptability is essential. You must be prepared to adjust your approach when destiny directs you down a different path. The detours destiny delivers are often defining moments that allow for development and growth. These deviations aren't derailments but opportunities to dive deeper into who you are and what you're destined to do. They demand resilience, but they also develop the depth of your character.

Destiny is not a predetermined path that dismisses your decisions. It's a design that develops over time, influenced by your daily actions and decisions. You decide how dedicated you are to your dreams, how determined you are to overcome difficulties, and how deeply you're willing to dive into your journey. Destiny, in return, directs the unfolding of your life, delivering you to destinations that may be different than you envisioned but ultimately more deserving of your devotion.

The delicate balance between destiny and decision-making demands a deep understanding of yourself. You must decide how much you're willing to dedicate to your dreams and how determined you are to drive through difficulties. Destiny delivers challenges, but it also directs you toward discoveries and destinations that are aligned with your deeper purpose.

Destiny is about development. It's the driving force behind who you're becoming. Every delay, every detour, every decision adds depth to your story. Even when disappointment dominates, destiny is still at work, developing you into the person you're destined to be.

In the end, destiny demands that you trust in the design of your life. It may not always be direct or devoid of difficulties, but it is always developing. Destiny directs your journey, defining your destination through every step you take, every decision you make, and every dream you dare to pursue. So, don't dread destiny.

Instead, dive into it, and let it deliver you to the destination that's truly deserving of your dedication and drive.

E

Effort
Giving Your Best

Effort is essential, an energy that elevates every endeavour you embark on. Every experience, every achievement, and every expectation requires effort. Effort is not an easy, everyday exercise; it's enduring, often extending far beyond initial enthusiasm. Whether you're eager to excel in education, eager to earn expertise in a new field, or eager to expand your horizons, effort is the engine that empowers you.

Effort is everything. Excellence, in essence, emerges from endless effort. Even extraordinary individuals have exerted enormous energy to earn their elite status. Look at athletes—examples of effort—who exercise endlessly, enduring exhausting routines, expending energy every single day. Without effort, their exceptional abilities would remain unrealized, their endeavours unfulfilled. They engage with an expectation that excellence isn't earned easily but instead evolves over extended timeframes. Even when exhausted, they extend their effort because they understand it's the only element that elevates them above everyone else.

Effort doesn't end when enthusiasm ebbs. It endures even when you encounter endless challenges or experience setbacks. Effort expects endurance. It's like an endless engine, essential for propelling you forward even when the journey feels eternal. Sometimes, it takes years of effort before you experience the excellence you envision. Effort isn't fleeting; it requires everyday engagement. No excellence emerges from mere ease. You need to embrace the idea that effort is extended, encompassing not just months but sometimes many years.

Even in education, effort is evident. Every excellent essay, every elevated exam score, and every enhanced skill requires extensive effort. Exams exemplify how effort elevates you. Endless evenings of engaging with texts, exhausting hours of studying, and exercising your mind endlessly lead to success. Effort, in education, ensures excellence over time.

Effort and energy are entwined; one fuels the other. You expend energy in each effort, engaging fully with every task. Whether you're enhancing your expertise, exploring a new element of your career, or even extending your empathy toward others, effort ensures that you evolve. Effort ensures expansion, ensuring that you exceed expectations and elevate your experiences to exceptional levels.

Even when effort doesn't immediately yield expected results, every exertion builds toward something bigger. Every small effort accumulates, every action echoes, and eventually, effort leads to excellence. Imagine an explorer in an endless desert. Every step might seem exhausting, but each one brings them closer to an eventual escape, an endpoint they may not yet envision. If they abandon effort, they would never experience the end of the journey. But by embracing effort, even through exhaustion, they ensure their eventual exit.

Effort isn't easy—it's exhausting, emotionally engaging, and, at times, exceedingly demanding. Yet, enduring effort ensures eventual success. Examples echo everywhere. Entrepreneurs, for instance, endure endless setbacks, but their effort eventually leads to extraordinary enterprises. Their efforts extend across endless evenings, evolving their dreams into endeavours that exceed their expectations. Even when the outcome feels elusive, effort ensures evolution. Every effort you extend moves you closer to your desired endpoint.

In essence, effort is the energy that empowers every excellence you endeavour to achieve. Enduring effort exceeds excitement, embracing the expectation that nothing excellent emerges effortlessly. Every example of success, excellence, or expertise you encounter exists because of effort—endless, exhaustive, and enduring effort. Whether it's earning an elite status in your field, expanding your education, or evolving your empathy for others, effort ensures that you not only exceed expectations but evolve into the person capable of excellence.

Effort, in every element, ensures that what you envision eventually emerges. It may take endless evenings, exhausting energy, or even extensive years, but effort will lead you to excellence every single time. Never underestimate the endless importance of effort. Embrace it, endure it, and evolve through it, knowing that effort is the element that ensures your excellence.

F

Focus

Focus On Goals

Focus fuels forward motion. It's the force that fastens your attention firmly on the future, framing your goals and freeing you from distractions. Focus, by its very definition, fosters fulfilment, yet finding and maintaining it feels far from simple. For many, focus falters when faced with fleeting distractions, frustrations, or fatigue. But focus, when fully embraced, forms the foundation for everything you aim to achieve.

Focus is fundamental in forging any form of success. Fixing your attention on what you want ensures that you funnel your energy in the right direction. For instance, think of focus like a flashlight in a fog-filled forest. Without focus, the path forward is faint, fragmented, and full of potential failure. But when you focus fully, that beam becomes fierce, cutting through the fog, illuminating the way, and fastening your feet firmly on the right track. Without focus, you're left floundering, fumbling through life without direction.

Firm focus requires formidable effort. It's not enough to feel focused for a fleeting moment; focus must flourish over time. Focus demands fortitude, the inner strength to fight off any force that might fragment your attention. Staying focused is like fastening yourself to a firm foundation—you're grounded in your goal, unshaken by any force that tries to pull you away.

Focused individuals forge forward despite fears and failures. Focus doesn't falter when faced with challenges; it fights for progress. Focus fixes your attention firmly on the final outcome, and it forges a path even when frustration or fatigue feels overwhelming. Focus fortifies your resolve. It's the force that refuses to let you fall into the trap of fleeting distractions or frustrations that could derail your forward movement. Focus functions as the friend that keeps you on course, focused on fulfilment, not failure.

Focus fosters progress. Without it, even the finest ideas fizzle before they flourish. Focus helps you filter out what's frivolous, allowing only what's essential to flow freely in your field of vision. With focus, you funnel your time, talent, and tenacity into what truly matters. For example, think of a farmer tending to their field. They focus on fertilising the soil, fostering growth, and filtering out weeds. If they fail to focus on what's important, their field falters. Focus, much like a farmer's work, ensures that your efforts flourish, free from distractions that could spoil the harvest of your hard work.

Focus isn't free from challenges, though. It faces fierce competitors—fear, frustration, fatigue, and even false expectations. Yet, with focus, you fend off these foes. Focus doesn't fold in the face of frustration or fatigue; it fortifies itself and finds ways to flourish even in the most challenging circumstances. Focus filters out fear and fixes your mind on the future you've fashioned for yourself.

The fact is, focus fuels everything. It fast-tracks you toward fulfilment and helps you forge a future filled with success. Without focus, you float aimlessly, failing to form firm footing toward your goals. But with focus, you can fearlessly face any obstacle, fortify your resolve, and filter out anything that would prevent you from flourishing.

Focus is the force that facilitates everything you hope to achieve. From forming your vision to following through, focus is fundamental. It's the flame that keeps you fired up, the frame that helps you filter out distractions, and the foundation upon which you build your future.

Focusing firmly on your future takes time, tenacity, and an unfailing commitment to forward motion. But once you foster that focus, the possibilities become far-reaching. Focus frees you from fears of failure, fastening you instead to the fulfilment that awaits at the finish line.

G

Growth
Learning and Evolving

Growth is a gradual journey, a genuine gift that grants you the ability to gain new ground and gather wisdom each day. Growing means grasping opportunities, gathering experiences, and giving yourself the grace to grow beyond your greatest goals. Growth isn't a goal you achieve once, it's an ongoing, evolving experience, guiding you through life's great challenges and giving you the grit to keep going.

Genuine growth doesn't happen in giant leaps, but in gradual gains. Each day gives you a new chance to grow, to gather knowledge, and to gain greater understanding. Growth is the gradual unfolding of your greatest potential. For instance, think of a garden—growth isn't immediate, it takes time. You need to give it care, to nurture it, allowing it to grow green and full. Growth is the same way. You give yourself time to gather new skills, grow your gifts, and give attention to areas that need growth. Each small gain builds toward something greater.

Growth guides you. It gives you goals to strive for and grants you the grace to accept that growth isn't always easy. Growth might come through grit and grind, through grappling with tough situations, but these growing pains are a good sign. They guide you to greater places. Growth doesn't guarantee a smooth journey, but it guarantees that you'll gain more wisdom, more grit, and a greater ability to handle life's challenges. Growth grants you the ability to get better, even when things get tough.

Growth is grounded in learning. The greatest gift growth gives you is the chance to gather lessons from your greatest gains and your gravest mistakes. Growth is about grasping the fact that learning never truly ends. Every experience is a gateway to growth, every mistake a lesson that guides you to greater heights. Growth gives you the ability to see failure not as the end, but as a gateway to something greater. It guides you to look beyond the gap between where you are and where you want to be. Growth grants you the gift of patience, allowing you to keep going, even when growth feels slow.

In life, growth grants you the gift of evolving into the best version of yourself. It's not about gaining everything at once, but about growing step by step. Growth is gradual, but with grit and determination, it brings you closer to your goals. Growth doesn't guarantee instant gratification, but it gives you the grit to keep going even when the going gets tough.

Growth is grounded in gratitude, too. Gratefulness gives you the mindset to appreciate the journey, to gather lessons from each step, and to give yourself credit for every gain you make, no matter how small. Growth happens when you acknowledge the good in every situation and give thanks for the gains, both big and small.

Growth is a gift that keeps giving. It guides you through life, helps you gather strength, and gives you the courage to keep going. Growing isn't about getting everything you want right away; it's about gaining greater understanding, gathering lessons from the grind, and giving yourself the grace to grow at your own pace. Growth grants you the ability to evolve, not just in what you do, but in who you are.

Growth is good—it's the greatest goal we can strive for. It's the gateway to greatness, guiding us through life's challenges, and giving us the grit and grace to keep going. So go ahead, give yourself the gift of growth. Keep going, keep growing, and gather all the good that comes from giving your all to your growth.

H

Hope
Believing in Possibilities

Hope is the heartbeat that hums within us, a hidden hand holding us up when the horizon seems hazy. Like a harbour in the storm, hope offers shelter from the harsh winds of hardship. It's the helm that helps us head toward happiness, even when hurdles lie ahead. Hope is like a healing herb—quiet, humble, yet potent, offering healing to hearts weighed down by doubt or despair.

Holding on to hope is like holding a handrail on a steep hill; it helps keep you steady when your footing falters. Hope hovers like the first hint of dawn after a heavy, haunting night. It whispers that, despite the hurdles, something brighter waits ahead. Just as heat melts ice, hope softens the hardness of hurt and heartbreak, helping you heal.

Hope has a humbling, yet heroic power. It hovers in the heart, even when everything else feels hollow. It doesn't require hard evidence, but simply the heartfelt belief that the future holds hidden treasures. Hope is like a hidden flame in the hearth, always flickering, waiting for a fresh gust of faith to help it glow brighter.

Harnessing hope is like holding a lantern in a dark hallway. You can't see the whole path, but it highlights just enough to help you take the next step. In the midst of hardship, hope hangs on, lighting up hidden paths, hinting that happiness is still possible. It's like hearing the hum of a song in the distance when silence feels overwhelming—a reminder that life, like music, holds harmonious moments ahead.

Hope helps us harness the strength we didn't know we had. It hums in our hearts like the steady rhythm of a drum, pushing us forward when we hesitate. It's like the hush that follows a heavy rainfall, the promise that the storm has passed, and new growth will soon begin. Hope plants seeds in the most hardened ground, holding the promise that, with time, they will hatch into something healthy and whole.

Like the horizon that holds the day in its arms, hope hugs our hearts, hinting that there's always more ahead. It's like the humble honeybee, tirelessly heading from flower to flower, harvesting sweetness from even the smallest of sources. Hope harvests happiness, even when it seems hidden, and helps us hang on when everything else feels hard.

Hope is like holding a kite high in the wind. You can't control the wind, but you hold the string, guiding it as best you can. Hope handles life's ups and downs with a light touch, helping us hover above hardship. It helps us handle hurt and hardship with grace, knowing that the winds will shift, and the highs will come again.

In the haze of hard times, hope is like the sun hidden behind heavy clouds—it hasn't disappeared, it's just waiting for the right moment to shine again. Hope is the hush before something new happens, the heartbeat that keeps us alive and alert, holding on for what's ahead.

Hope, like a harbour, shelters us when the seas of life are rough. It's the hum in the heart that says, "Hold on," even when happiness feels far away. Hope holds our hands, helping us head toward brighter horizons, and embrace the truth that possibilities always hover on the horizon, waiting for us to harness them.

Holding hope is like holding a hidden treasure—it may not always be visible, but it's there, a constant reminder that help, healing, and happiness are still ahead. Hope is the helping hand, the harbour, the humble hum that keeps us going, and the light that lifts us higher than we ever thought we could reach. So, hold on to hope—it's the horizon where all possibilities lie waiting.

I

Inspiration
Finding Motivation

Inspiration is like an invisible thread that interlaces itself through every instant, inviting us to ignite our inner drive. It's the initial spark that illuminates our imagination, the impulse that pushes us forward when inertia tries to hold us still. Inspiration is like the inhale before a leap—it fills you with the air of ambition and excitement, setting the stage for action. Without inspiration, our ideas would remain idle, but with it, we find the ignition needed to turn intent into initiative.

Imagine inspiration as the invisible ink that writes itself into the fabric of our lives. It's hidden at first, but with the right light, it becomes illuminated, allowing us to interpret its messages. Life, with its infinite intricacies, offers inspiration in unexpected instances. It's like finding a diamond in the dirt—sometimes you have to dig deep, but the brilliance is always waiting to be discovered. The beauty of inspiration is that it isn't finite; it flows freely, waiting for you to invite it in.

Inspiration is the inner impulse that ignites when we least expect it, like lightning that illuminates the night sky for a brief but brilliant moment. It invites us to inquire, to innovate, to involve ourselves more deeply in the moment. It's like a gentle invitation to imagine beyond the immediate, to see the infinite possibilities that life has in store. Inspiration insists that there's always something more, something new, something inviting on the horizon.

Inspiration, like the wind, is invisible, but its influence is immense. It may appear in the quietest moments—an idea sparked in the stillness, an insight that arrives like a whisper. Yet, it has the power to instil a sense of invincibility, as though with just a little inspiration, any impossibility can be overcome. It's like an internal instructor, guiding you toward invention and innovation, encouraging you to invest your energy in ideas that ignite your passion.

Inspiration is like an intricate puzzle, inviting you to investigate and piece together insights that seem intangible at first. It ignites curiosity, inviting you to imagine how the impossible can become inevitable. It's like climbing an incline, where each step upward feels like progress toward a goal that isn't always immediately visible. But inspiration insists that with every incline, there's a peak, a moment of clarity where all efforts align perfectly.

Inspiration injects itself into the simplest of sights, infusing them with insight and innovation. It's like watching the sunrise—at first, it's just light breaking the horizon, but with time, it fills the sky with intricate colours, inviting awe and admiration. Inspiration is like that; it infuses itself into your ideas, turning the ordinary into extraordinary. It insists on expanding your inner vision, pushing the limits of what you thought was possible.

Inspiration invites introspection, guiding you inward to investigate the depths of your desires and dreams. It's like a mirror, reflecting back what is inside, but with infinite interpretations. Every image, every idea, is a gateway to inspiration if we open ourselves to it. It ignites internal fires that had been merely embers, encouraging us to imagine new ways of interacting with the world, inspiring both innovation and intentionality.

Finally, inspiration is like a river that flows within us, infinite in its direction and depth. It winds through every part of our lives, influencing every instance, every interaction. Like water, it takes the shape of whatever container we place it in—be it work, art, or relationships. Inspiration isn't isolated to a single moment; it is interwoven into every day, infusing each one with infinite possibilities. With inspiration, we are invited to live intentionally, investing in our interests, and illuminating the infinite potential of every moment.

J

Journey
Embracing Your Path

The journey, just like a jagged jewel, is both joyous and jarring. It isn't just about the destination, but the jagged steps, the jumps over obstacles, and the junctions where choices are made. Each journey is unique, just as every jewel has its own shape and shine. The joy of the journey doesn't come from a smooth, straight path—it's the jagged edges, the jostling moments that give it character. Just like jewels need polishing, journeys shape and sharpen us as we go.

Just imagine jogging up a steep hill. Your legs feel the strain, the air gets thinner, and your body wants to stop, but with each step, there's a joy that jolts through your muscles. The journey feels tough, yet with every new stretch, you gain a better view. Life's journey is just like that jog—it's a mixture of hard climbs and breathtaking glimpses of joy. You may stumble or feel out of breath, but each step is a part of the journey toward something greater.

Journeys often jolt us in unexpected ways. Just as you think you're on a certain trajectory, life throws in a jarring turn. These moments, though jolting, are often the junctures where the most growth happens. Take, for example, a job you lose unexpectedly. At first, the jolt feels unjust, but soon after, you may jump into something even better—perhaps a passion project or a job that truly aligns with your joy. Journeys take us to places we don't always expect, but those jumps are part of what makes it beautiful.

Journeys are full of junctions where we need to choose our direction. These junctions can feel intimidating, like standing at the edge of a vast jungle, unsure of the way through. But these are the moments that inject the journey with excitement and meaning. Life gives us junctions—like choosing a career, a place to live, or even a partner—and these decisions shape the journey ahead. Though the path isn't always clear, it's the act of choosing that adds richness to the experience.

Joys and jolts go hand in hand on this journey. Just as the ocean's waves rise and fall, so too does life. One moment, you might be riding high on a wave of joy, and the next, a jarring wave of struggle might hit you. Yet, just as the ocean is constant, the journey keeps going. Every joy you experience is amplified by the jarring moments that preceded it. Imagine finally achieving a goal after years of juggling different jobs or juggling family responsibilities—the joy is sweeter because of the journey.

Journeys are also about joining hands with others. Just as a jungle is dense and wild, it's easier to navigate when you journey with others. Joining forces with friends, family, or even strangers on the same path can make the journey less jarring and more joyful. Life is full of moments where we get to journey together—whether it's through shared challenges or joint celebrations. Just like joy multiplies when shared, so does the strength to handle the jarring parts of the journey.

Journeys involve jumping into the unknown. Just as a river journeys through valleys and over rocks, we too must jump into situations we've never encountered before. These jumps might seem risky, but they are often the parts of the journey that lead to the most growth. Just like a river finds its way through the jagged landscape, so do we, jumping from one challenge to another, navigating the jagged edges until we reach smoother waters.

Finally, every journey, no matter how jarring or joyful, leaves a jewel of wisdom. It's like a journey through a dense jungle—along the way, you might collect scars from the branches, but you also collect stories, skills, and wisdom. Each journey, with its jumps, jolts, and joys, is a jagged gem that shapes us into who we are meant to be. As we journey through life, we just have to embrace the jarring moments, knowing that they add to the overall beauty of the path ahead.

K

Kindness

Spreading Positivity

Kindness is a kingly quality, keeping the world connected like a kingdom ruled by warmth and care. It's like a key that unlocks the hearts of those you meet, and with each kind act, you kindle a fire that keeps the coldness of life away. Imagine kindness as a knight, gallant and noble, knocking away negativity and carrying the banner of goodwill wherever it goes. The beauty of kindness is that it never weakens—each kind word, each kind gesture, only strengthens it further.

Keeping kindness in your heart is like holding a kite that catches the strongest winds. As it soars higher, the sky clears, and everyone below feels the joy. Every kind act is like adding another knot to the string, making the kite more resilient and steady, allowing it to reach even greater heights. Just like a kite on a windy day, kindness knows no limits. It can go far beyond what you ever imagined, reaching into the lives of others and lifting them up when they least expect it.

Kindness is a key that, once turned, opens up a kingdom of possibilities. It doesn't just unlock doors; it breaks down walls, allowing connections to form in even the most unlikely places. Imagine kindness as a magic key, turning effortlessly in locks that seemed jammed with years of bitterness. Suddenly, everything opens up, and a flood of warmth and understanding flows in. It's like discovering a hidden kingdom of care that had been waiting just behind a closed door.

Kindness kicks away cruelty like a knight swinging his sword in battle, cutting through the darkest of days with just a single action. One act of kindness can feel like a knock on the door of someone's heart, waking them up to the possibility of a better day. Think of kindness as the strongest knight in shining armour, always on the move, ready to jump in and defend those in need. It's not just a small thing—it's a force that can change the course of someone's entire life.

Kindness is like a kaleidoscope, shifting and changing, yet always beautiful. Each new act adds another colourful piece to the pattern, and the more kindness you show, the more intricate the design becomes. Imagine looking through a kaleidoscope and seeing kindness reflected in every direction—every angle shows a new way to connect with others, to lift them up, to make the world a little bit brighter. Kindness keeps turning, keeps creating new ways to surprise and delight those around you.

Keeping kindness at the core of who you are is like wearing a cloak that protects not just you, but everyone you meet. It wraps around you like a soft, warm fabric, and as you move through life, you offer that warmth to others. Imagine walking through a cold, windy day, but each time you encounter someone, you give them a piece of your cloak, and they, too, are warmed by it. Kindness doesn't lessen as you share it—it grows, like a fire that spreads to keep more and more people safe from the cold.

Kindness is the king of qualities, and it commands respect without ever asking for it. It's like a quiet king who never raises his voice, yet everyone listens. When you act with kindness, it's as though you're carrying a royal decree that people can't help but follow. They respond in kind, and before long, the whole kingdom is filled with the warmth of mutual care and respect. Just like a king leads by example, your acts of kindness can inspire others to follow your lead.

In the grand journey of life, kindness is like the compass that keeps you on the right path. It doesn't matter how far off course you may feel—kindness can kick you back in the right direction. Imagine being lost in a forest, but with each kind gesture, a new path opens up before you, leading you out of the darkness and into the light. Kindness is the guide that keeps you grounded, no matter how chaotic life may become. It's the key to happiness, the knight that fights for what's right, and the kingdom where everyone is welcome.

L

Leadership Guiding Yourself & Others

Leadership is like a lighthouse, lighting the path for those who follow. Leading others means letting yourself be the light, the one people look to when the way forward seems lost. Leaders don't just lead with loud commands or large gestures; they live by example, letting their actions speak louder than their words. Living as a leader means learning daily, listening intently, and lifting others up when life feels heavy. Leadership lies in love for what you do, and loyalty to the people you guide.

Leaders are like ladders, allowing others to climb higher. Think of a leader you admire—likely, they didn't just focus on lifting themselves. They looked at how they could lift others, too. Leadership isn't a lone journey; it's a long-lasting legacy that leaves a lasting impact. By learning the needs of the people you lead, you become like a link in a long chain of growth and success, helping everyone you guide level up in life.

Live leadership isn't about loud leadership. It's about leading with a calm, clear purpose. Like a lion silently surveying the landscape, a leader listens before acting.

Live examples of leadership are all around us—look at local leaders like teachers, who lead with lessons, love, and patience, or community leaders who lend their time and talents to make local lives better. Leaders don't always wear labels; sometimes, leadership lurks in the little things they do daily.

Leading is like laying the foundation for a lasting legacy. You learn along the way, sometimes from losses, sometimes from laughter. A leader learns to live with both. A live example of this would be athletes—look at Lionel Messi, who leads with his love for the game and lets his passion lift his team. He doesn't just live for his own glory; his leadership is about loyalty to his team, leading them to victory through lessons learned on the field.

Listening is a leader's lifeline. It lets leaders link with those they guide, learning from their lives, loves, and losses. In leadership, listening is like holding a mirror up to the lives of others—it reflects their needs, allowing you to lead them more effectively. A live example of this can be seen in leaders like Malala Yousafzai, who listens to the voices of girls globally and leads by lifting their stories to the world stage.

Leaders live by lifting the limitations of others, allowing them to learn and grow. Leadership is less about laying down rules and more about letting others find their light. Like a leaf turning toward the sunlight, people naturally lean toward leaders who let them live and learn freely. Think of leaders like Elon Musk, whose leadership leans on letting innovation and ideas lead the way. He lifts the limits on what people think is possible, and through that, leads them to new levels of achievement.

Leadership is layered. It's not linear—it's full of loops and lessons. Sometimes, you lose, and sometimes, you land right where you're supposed to be. Live examples of this can be seen in leaders like Steve Jobs, who lived through losses and leveraged them into lessons. He let each setback lead him to new insights, and in doing so, laid the foundation for his lasting legacy. Leadership, like life, is full of twists, but a leader learns to live through them all.

Leaders leave a lasting mark on the lives they touch. Like a lantern lighting the way, they guide others through life's darkest corners, leading not by force but by love, loyalty, and learning. Live leadership is about letting others lean on you when needed, but also letting them learn to stand tall on their own. Like the leaders who lift others daily, your leadership will live on in the lives you touch, making the world a little lighter and a little lovelier with each lesson you leave behind.

M

Motivation
The Drive That Pushes You

Motivation is the motor that moves you toward your goals. It's the magic that makes mundane moments meaningful and magnifies your purpose. Many might misunderstand motivation as a momentary mood, but it's much more. Motivation is the mental mindset that maintains your momentum. When you're motivated, nothing seems impossible; mountains become molehills, and what once might've felt monstrous becomes manageable.

Most people might mistake motivation for mere motivation quotes or motivational talks. But motivation is more than that. It's the mastery of your mind, moulding your mindset into something magnificent. Think of motivation like music—sometimes, it's mellow, barely noticeable in the background, but it's always there. Other times, it's mighty, moving you forward with full force. You just need to find the melody that moves you.

Maintaining motivation, however, might sometimes feel like a marathon. There are moments when it's easy to lose momentum. But remember, motivation is a muscle—you must maintain it. The more you work on it, the more it grows. Like marathon runners making it mile by mile, motivation requires mental strength, consistency, and most of all, determination. Motivation will move you even when the road ahead feels messy or misty.

Mastering motivation means making the most of your mindset. Much like a map guiding you to your destination, motivation maps out the steps you need to take. You might not always see the final milestone, but motivation helps you focus on making that next move. Making progress, no matter how minimal, matters. Even when things seem murky or you meet obstacles, motivation pushes you to make adjustments and move forward.

Many find motivation in moments of meaning. Maybe it's a memory, a milestone, or a meaningful message from someone who matters to you. These moments multiply your motivation, helping you manage the struggles that might come your way. Remember, motivation doesn't magically manifest itself—you must be mindful of it. You must make space for it in your daily life and let it multiply through meaningful actions.

Motivation also thrives in momentum. Moving forward, even in small steps, can make all the difference. The more you move, the more motivated you become. Imagine motivation like a moving machine—the more fuel you give it, the faster and further it goes. Every move you make matters. Even if it's just one small step, it contributes to maintaining your momentum.

Sometimes, motivation might feel masked. Maybe the mission seems massive, or the path seems muddled. But motivation helps you manage those moments. When the mission feels mighty, break it into manageable steps. Let motivation be your guide, reminding you that many small moves make a massive difference. Motivation is always there, like a hidden magnet pulling you forward, even when you might not immediately notice it.

Motivation is more than just a feeling—it's the force that makes you move. It's the mental muscle that gives meaning to your moments and helps you maintain momentum through life's many challenges. Make sure to nourish it, nurture it, and never let it melt away. Let motivation move you toward making the most of your life, no matter the obstacles.

N

Never Give Up
Persistence In The KEY

Never giving up is the necessary key to navigating life's numerous challenges. No matter how narrow the path may seem or how negative the noise around you gets, you need to nurture a never-ending sense of persistence. It's natural to feel nervous when things aren't moving as planned, but never let negativity nest in your mind. Remember, nothing worth achieving ever comes easily; the night is darkest just before the new dawn.

Nurturing a never-quit mentality is like nurturing a seed. Not every day will be filled with notable growth, but with nourishment, the seed will eventually sprout. Persistence is the nourishment you need to nurture your goals. The necessary ingredient for success is not talent or luck; it's the notion that, no matter how many times you fall, you will get up again and again.

Think of the nobility in nature—look at the mighty oak tree, which starts from a tiny nut. It never questions its ability to grow tall, even when the nights are long and the storms are strong. The tree knows that growth takes time and tenacity. Likewise, in your journey, every knock should be seen as a nudge toward your next opportunity. Never let yourself think that a no today means a never—it might just mean "not yet."

No one reaches new heights without navigating through a net of naysayers. Whether it's friends, family, or even the nagging voice in your own head, negativity will nibble at your confidence. Nevertheless, you must nurture resilience and neutralise these negative notions. Take Nelson Mandela, for instance. Nearly three decades in prison didn't nullify his dreams or negate his hope for a nation united by equality. His persistence was a notable force that reshaped history.

In life, not everything will neatly fall into place. There will be nuisances and nosedives. However, the next step is always nearer than you think. Like navigating through a maze, persistence will eventually lead you to an opening. Never forget that even when the road feels non-existent, a single step forward can make all the difference. The journey may not be neat, but each new turn brings new possibilities.

Nourish the narrative that failure is just a necessary note in the song of success. Many notable names—Nikola Tesla, for instance—experienced numerous failures before reaching groundbreaking success. But they never let failure become their final chapter. Each no was simply another notch in their belt, another step toward mastering their craft. You must nurture this same mentality, recognizing that persistence is the only way to navigate the labyrinth of life.

Never underestimate the power of a never-give-up attitude. Persistence is like a navigator guiding you through the unknown. You may not know exactly where you're headed, but your determination ensures that you'll get there nonetheless. Like a navigator relying on the stars in the night sky, you must rely on your inner drive to push through the obstacles. No matter how far off course you feel, persistence will guide you back on track.

In conclusion, nothing is more powerful than the notion of never giving up. It's the needle that stitches together success from the fabric of failure. Whether in small endeavours or enormous life goals, you need to nurture persistence at every turn. Remember, no challenge is too great when you've got the necessary persistence in your heart. Stay true to the belief that every "no" leads to a new "next." Keep moving, and never let go of the notion that success is near.

O

Opportunity
Recognizing Opportunities

Opportunity often opens doors to the unknown, offering a chance to overcome obstacles and outgrow old limitations. Often overlooked or obscured by obstacles, opportunities are omnipresent if you open your mind to them. Opportunity operates as a key, unlocking paths to growth and success, but only if you're observant and open to its offerings. Like an open ocean, full of endless possibilities, the key to opportunity is learning to navigate its often unpredictable waves.

One obvious truth about opportunity is that it doesn't always arrive with obvious signs. Often, it's obscure, hidden within obstacles or ordinary moments. Imagine an opportunity as an orchard—each opportunity is an orange hanging from a branch, but you must climb to reach it. The climb may seem overwhelming at first, but once you obtain that orange, the reward is obvious. Opportunities, much like fruit, often grow in the soil of obstacles, sprouting where others overlook.

Opportunities aren't always one-size-fits-all. Some come in overwhelming waves, while others are overlooked because they're obscured by our own outlook. Take someone like Oprah, who grew up facing overwhelming odds but saw each obstacle as an opportunity to overcome and outshine her circumstances. Her outlook on life opened doors to outstanding achievements, and she turned her obstacles into opportunities for growth, much like a flower breaking through concrete.

Opening your mind to opportunity requires optimism. Often, we miss out on opportunities because we focus on the obstacles. But optimism allows you to see obstacles as opportunities in disguise. Picture opportunity as a door—optimism is the key that opens it. Without it, we'd only see the locked door, not the possibility that lies beyond. Optimism overpowers doubt, allowing you to overlook the difficulties and focus on the growth awaiting on the other side.

Observing opportunities requires openness, a willingness to step outside your comfort zone and embrace the unknown. Opportunities often originate from ordinary moments but offer outstanding growth if you opt to seize them. Think of an inventor like Thomas Edison, who saw every obstacle as an opportunity to optimise his inventions. He observed, learned, and operated with the mindset that every failure offered insight for future success.

Opportunities can also operate like oars, helping you row your boat through the ocean of life. Without them, you're adrift, but with them, you can orient yourself toward your goals. The ocean may be vast and open, but without oars—without opportunities—you're left floating without direction. Each opportunity offers you the chance to row toward your destination, allowing you to overcome the odds and reach your goals.

Often, opportunity operates on its own timeline. It doesn't always arrive when we expect it or in the form we imagine. However, being open to its offerings ensures that when it does come, you're ready to obtain it. Picture an oyster—opportunity is like the pearl inside. You may need to open several oysters before you find the gem inside, but the effort is always worth it. Opportunities often hide beneath layers, waiting to be uncovered.

In the end, opportunities are ongoing. They don't only arrive once but occur over time, offering ongoing chances to optimise your life. Observing them, being open to them, and operating with optimism ensures that you won't overlook them. Like a garden, opportunities grow when you nurture them, allowing you to bloom into your full potential. Obstacles may obstruct the way, but with an open mind, you'll always find opportunities waiting to be seized.

P

Passion
Pouring Your Heart

Passion is the powerful pulse that propels you forward, pushing you to pour your heart into every project, every plan, and every purpose. People who pursue passion possess a profound energy that propels them beyond mere practicality. Passion provides the power to persist, even when the path seems perplexing or packed with problems. It's the fire that fuels progress, turning potential into performance.

Picture passion as a plant that, when properly nurtured, grows and thrives. It starts with a single seed—perhaps an idea, a hobby, or a profession—and with persistent care, it blossoms into something beautiful and productive. Like a plant, passion requires patience and protection. It may not produce results immediately, but with purposeful effort, it will eventually flourish.

Passion pushes people past their perceived limits. Take athletes, for instance—professional players pour their entire purpose into practice, perfecting their performance because passion drives them to play at their peak. Passion primes them to push through pain, past fatigue, and beyond failure. Without passion, progress would pause, and potential would remain unexplored.

Passion isn't passive; it's proactive. It prompts you to pursue possibilities, even when the payoff isn't guaranteed. Passionate people persist through pressure, propelled by their personal attachment to the process. Think of passionate performers—painters, poets, performers on stage—each pour their personalities into their work, producing something that resonates with others because it reflects their passion.

Purpose and passion go hand in hand. Your passion is often linked to your purpose in life, and following that passion can lead to profound personal growth. Passion provides you with a sense of direction, helping you prioritise what's important and push aside what's peripheral. Like a compass pointing you toward the true north, passion points you toward your purpose, keeping you on the path to personal fulfilment.

Passion also promotes perseverance. When you're passionate about something, you're more likely to persevere through problems and pitfalls. You won't be easily discouraged or disheartened because passion keeps the fire burning. It's the persistent push that helps you power through difficulties, staying the course until you reach the pinnacle of your potential. Passion prepares you for the long haul, helping you maintain your focus even when progress seems slow.

People who possess passion often attract others who share similar pursuits. Passion is like a magnet, pulling people toward a shared purpose. Whether it's in personal relationships or professional partnerships, passion creates powerful connections. People naturally gravitate toward those who display passion because it's inspiring and infectious. Passion projects positivity, and that energy permeates everything around it.

In the end, passion is the pulse of life. It's what propels you to pursue your dreams with persistence and pride. It's what makes the journey worth it, turning every step into a purposeful stride. Passion is the force that propels you from potential to achievement, from plans to progress, and from possibility to reality. So pour your heart into what you do, and let passion pave the path to your personal and professional peak.

Q

Quality
Quest For Excellence

Quality is a quintessential quest, quickly qualifying qualities that quantify excellence. Quietly, quality quells questionable queries, quenching qualms and cultivating clarity. Quality pursuits quickly yield quintessential outcomes, showcasing the quest for exceptional results.

Qualitative efforts, whether in work or relationships, produce quantifiable results. Quality enhances credibility, ensuring you stand out in a crowded field of quality-quenched competitors. You'll acquire respect and recognition rapidly when you prioritise quality over quantity. Quality not only cultivates satisfaction but also attracts qualified opportunities, establishing you as a go-to person in your field.

Quality requires questioning. You must frequently ask yourself, "Is this the best I can do?" "Am I settling for less?" Questing for quality means acquiring knowledge and continuously questioning the status quo. It demands an openness to critique and a willingness to adjust your approach based on feedback. When you commit to quality, you become more aware of the intricacies that can elevate your work from mediocre to magnificent.

In this quest, quality acts as a quick key to success, but it's not always a quick fix. Achieving quality requires diligence, discipline, and a deep understanding of what excellence entails. Think of quality as a fine wine; it takes time to cultivate, ferment, and perfect. When you focus on quality, you are engaging in a continuous process of refinement, learning from experiences, and adjusting your methods accordingly.

Moreover, cultivating quality in your life leads to profound personal growth. Quality influences your daily decisions and interactions, guiding you toward better outcomes. It encourages you to choose projects and relationships that resonate with your values. Whether it's crafting a product, leading a team, or nurturing friendships, quality should be the guiding principle in all pursuits. Quality fosters trust, ensuring you're seen as a reliable, reputable individual.

Let's not forget that quality can often lead to unexpected opportunities. When you consistently deliver high-quality work, you create a reputation that opens doors you never knew existed. People are drawn to quality, and when they see it, they want to be a part of it. Whether it's through referrals, collaborations, or

new projects, the quest for quality can lead you to paths you never imagined.
Finally, remember that quality isn't just about the end result; it's also about the journey. Embracing quality means engaging with the process, appreciating each step, and learning from every experience. Each challenge is an opportunity to refine your approach and improve your skills. Quality should be your compass, guiding you through the complexities of life and work.

In conclusion, quality is the quintessential factor that drives success. By embracing a quality-centric approach, you create a legacy of excellence that resonates through your work and life. So, commit to the quest for quality, and watch as it transforms not only your achievements but also your perspective on what is possible.

R

Resilience

Bouncing Back from Setbacks

Resilience represents our remarkable ability to recover from rigorous challenges. Rarely does life proceed smoothly; rather, it regularly presents roadblocks and rigorous trials that require remarkable resolve. Resilience isn't merely a response; it's a resource that we can harness, refining our reactions to adversity and reinforcing our strength.

Reflecting on your recovery from past setbacks reveals the roots of your resilience. Remember a rough time when you faced real hardship? Perhaps you felt reduced or restricted. Yet, recognizing how you rebounded reveals your inner reservoir of strength. Resilience requires recognizing your capacity to recover, reminding you that each rough patch can lead to renewed resolve and readiness for future endeavours.

Resilience is often reinforced by relationships. Surrounding yourself with reassuring friends and supportive family members can create a robust network. Relationships can reinforce your recovery process, reminding you that you're never really alone.

Each encouraging word and each supportive gesture acts as a reinforcement, empowering your resolve to rise again after facing difficulties.

Moreover, resilience often requires a re-evaluation of your reactions. Instead of reacting with resistance to discomfort, recognize that these experiences can enrich your resilience. Adapting your response to challenges involves reframing your mindset; viewing each setback as an opportunity for growth rather than a roadblock. It's about transforming regret into resolve and disappointment into determination.

Regular practices can also reinforce resilience. Activities such as meditation, journaling, or physical exercise recharge your emotional battery. These rituals not only provide restorative moments but also help you reconnect with your inner self. By reinforcing positive habits, you prepare yourself to react more resilient when faced with future challenges. Consistency in these routines can rejuvenate your spirit and reinforce your commitment to personal growth.

Remember, resilience is not solely about bouncing back; it's about rising even stronger than before. When recurring challenges arise, remind yourself that every setback equips you with renewed resources and perspectives. Each experience, whether good or bad, can serve as a stepping stone, not just a stumbling block. Resilience thrives when you reprocess experiences, transforming past pains into powerful lessons.

Recognizing and celebrating your achievements plays a crucial role in fostering resilience. Acknowledging every recovery, no matter how small, reinforces your determination to keep moving forward. This reflective practice creates a positive feedback loop, encouraging you to embrace new challenges with a courageous spirit. Each moment of recognition reinforces your resilience and inspires others around you.

In conclusion, resilience is an essential quality that empowers you to recover from setbacks and confront life's challenges. By reflecting on past experiences, nurturing supportive relationships, and engaging in regular practices, you can cultivate resilience and embrace growth. So, the next time life throws a challenge your way, remember your capacity to rise again. Embrace your resilience, recognizing that you have the strength to confront and overcome any obstacle.

S

Strength

Finding Power Within Yourself

Strength signifies a special power residing within you. Some see strength as simply physical prowess, but true strength surpasses mere muscle. It stems from self-belief, self-awareness, and the ability to stand steadfast amidst storms. Strength should be celebrated, for it's a source of solace and support in trying times.

Sometimes, strength surfaces during significant struggles. When faced with setbacks or stressors, it's essential to summon that inner strength. Self-reflection can serve as a starting point for this process. Take a step back, assess your situation, and silence self-doubt. Strength arises from understanding that challenges shape your character, building resilience and self-sufficiency.

Surrounding yourself with supportive individuals also fosters strength. Seek relationships that spark positivity and encouragement. Friends and family who celebrate your successes and stand by you during struggles are vital to sustaining your strength. Strong connections enhance your ability to persevere, reminding you that you're not alone in your journey.

Furthermore, self-care plays a significant role in sustaining your strength. Taking time to nourish your mind, body, and spirit is crucial. Simple acts such as savoring a soothing tea, stretching, or soaking in a warm bath can restore your sense of well-being. Prioritising self-care is not selfish; it's a necessary step in reinforcing your strength.

Additionally, setting small, achievable goals can solidify your sense of strength. Start with simple tasks, slowly building toward more substantial challenges. Each small success serves as a stepping stone, strengthening your confidence. Celebrate these milestones, for each one signifies progress and the power to persist.

Strength also emerges from learning and self-improvement. Strive to seek knowledge and skills that enhance your capabilities. Embrace setbacks as opportunities for growth. A strong mindset acknowledges that mistakes are stepping stones toward success. By shifting your perspective, you transform challenges into learning experiences that strengthen your resolve.

Moreover, storytelling can illuminate your strength. Share your experiences with others, inspiring them to recognize their strength within. Stories serve as powerful reminders that everyone faces struggles and that resilience is a shared human experience. By expressing your journey, you not only affirm your strength but also foster connections that enrich your life and the lives of others.

In conclusion, strength is not just about physical power; it's a profound force that lies within each of us. By understanding and embracing your strength, you can navigate life's challenges with confidence and grace. Cultivate self-awareness, nurture supportive relationships, prioritise self-care, and pursue personal growth. Remember, the strength you seek is already within you, waiting to be unleashed. So, step forward, summon your strength, and shine brightly through every storm you face.

T

Tenacity

Holding On Until You Succeed

Tenacity refers to a tireless determination to triumph, no matter the trials you face. This trait is crucial; tenacity fuels the fire within, pushing you to tackle challenges head-on. It's that tenacious spirit that tells you to keep going, to trust in your journey, and to never throw in the towel. If you tap into tenacity, you can transform trials into triumphs.

Time and time again, tenacity proves its importance. Think about those tough times when you felt tempted to throw in the towel. Maybe you tackled a tricky task at work or attempted to train for a marathon. Each time you felt the tug of doubt, your tenacity shone through. You turned trials into triumphs, teaching yourself that persistence pays off, no matter how tough the journey seems.

To cultivate tenacity, take time to set tangible targets. Clearly defined goals can help you track your progress, keeping you motivated along the way. Instead of tackling a towering task all at once, break it into tiny, attainable steps. Each tiny triumph builds your confidence, reinforcing your tenacity and reminding you that every effort counts.

Taking time to reflect on past triumphs can also strengthen your tenacity. Recall a time when you faced tough obstacles but triumphed through sheer determination. Trust that those experiences are testaments to your tenacity. Every trial you've tackled teaches valuable lessons, solidifying your belief that you can overcome any situation that comes your way.

Tenacity often requires a strong mindset. Train your thoughts to focus on positive affirmations rather than doubts. Instead of thinking, "I can't do this," transform that thought into, "I will tackle this task, step by step." This mental shift is crucial in nurturing your tenacity. Surround yourself with supportive people who inspire you and reinforce your tenacity, fostering a positive environment that encourages growth.

Tools for tenacity include techniques for maintaining your energy and enthusiasm. Engage in activities that ignite your passions and interests. Whether it's participating in a thrilling sport, immersing yourself in a creative project, or volunteering for a worthy cause, these activities keep your spirit alive. Tenacity thrives when you're fully engaged and excited about your journey, making every step feel like a thrill rather than a chore.

Time can also be a great teacher of tenacity. Understand that true success doesn't happen overnight. It takes time, effort, and unwavering commitment to turn dreams into reality. Trust the process, even when it feels tedious or tiring. The tenacious mindset understands that every tick of the clock is a step toward triumph, and each moment spent working toward your goals is a testament to your resolve.

In conclusion, tenacity is the unwavering strength that propels you forward, even when faced with tough times. Embrace the challenges you encounter, and trust in your ability to triumph. Cultivate a strong mindset, set tangible targets, and reflect on past successes to strengthen your determination. Remember, every effort counts, and tenacity will ultimately lead you to the success you seek. So, hold tight to your dreams, stay true to your goals, and let your tenacity shine through every challenge.

U

Understanding

Knowing Yourself and Others

Understanding unlocks unique insights into ourselves and others. It's that undeniable urge to grasp the intricacies of feelings, thoughts, and behaviours. When you seek understanding, you unleash a universe of opportunities for connection and growth. It's essential to cultivate this understanding, not just for personal development but also for nurturing meaningful relationships.

To truly understand yourself, embark on an unfolding journey of self-discovery. Uncover your values, your passions, and your unique traits. Ask yourself the tough questions: What do I truly want? What makes me feel fulfilled? Understanding these aspects is crucial, as they serve as your guiding principles. Use journaling or meditation to facilitate this unfolding process, allowing your subconscious to unveil hidden truths.

Equally important is understanding others. Each individual you encounter brings a unique story, shaped by their experiences and emotions. When you approach interactions with curiosity, you begin to unearth the layers of their humanity. Instead of making assumptions, utilise active listening. This practice allows you to understand others on a deeper level, promoting empathy and compassion in your relationships.

Understanding requires a willingness to suspend judgement. It's all too easy to jump to conclusions based on superficial observations. However, true understanding involves looking beyond the surface. It encourages us to unearth the underlying motivations and struggles that shape behaviours. By fostering an unbiased attitude, you open yourself up to richer, more meaningful connections with those around you.

Utilize effective communication as a tool for understanding. Words are powerful, and how we express ourselves can significantly impact our relationships. Strive for clarity in your communication, ensuring your thoughts and feelings are understood. Equally, encourage others to share their perspectives without fear of misunderstanding. This exchange cultivates a deeper mutual understanding, enhancing connections between individuals.

In moments of misunderstanding or conflict, remember the importance of patience. Sometimes, misunderstandings can lead to frustrations or unresolved tensions. Instead of reacting impulsively, take a moment to breathe and reflect. Understanding takes time, and approaching conflicts with a calm demeanour can help you uncover the root of the issue. Use these moments as opportunities for growth rather than division.

Your understanding will evolve over time, as you encounter new experiences and individuals. Embrace this continuous journey of learning. Each interaction holds the potential to teach you something new about yourself and the world around you. Be open to adapting your understanding, allowing it to shift and grow as you navigate life's challenges and joys.

Ultimately, understanding serves as a bridge that connects us to ourselves and each other. It enriches our lives, offering insights and fostering empathy. By committing to the practice of understanding, you create a more compassionate and harmonious environment for yourself and those around you. So, take the time to explore, engage, and connect with the understanding that is essential for a fulfilling life.

V

Vision
Future You Want to Create

Vision is vital; it's the vibrant view of the future you wish to create. It serves as a powerful vehicle that drives your desires and decisions. Without a vivid vision, life can feel like a vague voyage without a destination. When you visualise your goals, you provide yourself with a framework to navigate toward the future you envision.

To develop your vision, start by identifying your values and aspirations. Ask yourself, "What do I truly value?" Visualising your values is crucial. For example, consider a visionary like Steve Jobs. His vision for Apple was rooted in values of innovation and creativity. By vividly picturing a world with beautifully designed technology, he transformed his vision into reality, launching products that revolutionised industries.

Next, practise vibrant visualisation techniques. Picture your ideal scenario. If your vision involves becoming a successful musician, imagine yourself on stage, performing in front of a vibrant audience. Feel the energy, the excitement, and the applause. This mental imagery can invigorate your drive. As you visualise, channel that energy into your daily routine, ensuring every action aligns with your vision.

However, vision alone isn't enough; you need vigorous action. Without action, your vision remains a mere fantasy. Take small steps toward your goal daily. If you aspire to be an author, commit to writing regularly, even if just a few vibrant paragraphs each day. Remember, every step forward, no matter how small, contributes to the larger vision. Persistence is vital in this journey.

Vigilance is another key component. Stay alert to opportunities that align with your vision. The world is full of variables; adaptability can make a significant difference. Think about how visionary leaders like Jeff Bezos have adjusted their strategies based on changing market conditions. Their ability to pivot while remaining true to their core vision has led to immense success. Keep your eyes open to shifts that could enhance your path.

Validation from others can further strengthen your vision. Share your ideas with supportive friends or mentors who can provide feedback. Their perspectives can add valuable insights and reinforce your belief in your vision. For instance, J.K. Rowling faced numerous rejections before her vision for Harry Potter became a global phenomenon. Her persistence, paired with encouragement from friends, helped her achieve what seemed impossible.

Vibrancy in your environment can also enhance your vision. Surround yourself with inspiring individuals and materials that resonate with your goals. Create a vision board filled with images and quotes that spark joy and motivation. Think of how vibrant communities, like those of artists or entrepreneurs, can invigorate your spirit and fuel your vision. Engaging with like-minded individuals will help maintain your momentum.

In conclusion, your vision is a vital force that propels you toward your desired future. By visualising your goals, taking vigorous action, remaining vigilant, seeking validation, and surrounding yourself with vibrancy, you can transform your aspirations into reality. Embrace the journey ahead, and remember that your vision is the guiding light illuminating your path. Keep your vision vivid, your actions vigorous, and your spirit vibrant as you move toward the future you wish to create.

W

Wisdom
Learning From Experience

Wisdom is a wondrous wealth we wield through the winding ways of life. It's that warm, wise quality that wraps around our experiences, whispering valuable lessons that we wouldn't want to overlook. Without wisdom, we wander through life's wilderness, unaware of the wealth of insights waiting to be witnessed. By learning from every experience, we water the seeds of wisdom, watching them grow into a profound understanding of the world around us.

When we welcome worthwhile experiences, whether wins or woes, we begin to weave wisdom into our lives. Consider the wise words of Walt Disney, who once said, "We keep moving forward, opening new doors, and doing new things." His journey was a whirlwind of wondrous creativity, and he wisely turned every setback into a stepping stone for success. With each whimsical project, he wove together lessons learned, ultimately building an empire that continues to inspire wonder worldwide.

Watching wise mentors walk through their journeys can also pave the way for our wisdom. Seek out individuals who have weathered life's storms with grace. Take, for instance, the legendary environmentalist Wangari Maathai, who waged a war for sustainable development and women's rights. After facing numerous challenges, including political opposition, she emerged wiser and more determined. With her unwavering commitment to the environment, she founded the Green Belt Movement, advocating for tree planting and women's empowerment worldwide, making waves in a world often resistant to change.

Writing down our thoughts and reflections can further awaken our wisdom. Journaling provides a window into our minds, allowing us to witness our growth and weave our stories into a coherent narrative. Writers like Willa Cather have shown that written words wield tremendous power. Through her writing, she shared the warmth of human experiences, weaving wisdom into her characters' journeys, inspiring countless readers to find their own voices.

Wisdom often requires a willingness to learn from every wretched mistake. When we stumble, it's easy to wallow in worries and regrets. Instead, let's embrace those moments as opportunities for growth. Take, for example, the wise words of Winston Churchill: "Success is stumbling from failure to failure with no loss of enthusiasm." His wisdom lies in his ability to learn and rise from each setback, ultimately leading the

world through turbulent times with unwavering resolve.
Moreover, wise individuals possess the ability to weigh their options and consider the wider consequences before making decisions. This thoughtful approach allows them to navigate the web of life's complexities with wonder. Look at Warren Buffett, widely regarded as the wisest investor. His wisdom is evident in how he waits for the right opportunities and wisely assesses risks, ensuring that his wealth grows steadily over time.

Working collaboratively with others can also enhance our wisdom. Engaging in worthwhile discussions and exchanging ideas with diverse perspectives broadens our understanding of the world. Workshops that bring together willing participants often foster wisdom through shared experiences. These gatherings not only promote learning but also strengthen bonds, creating a wonderful community where wisdom flourishes.

Finally, wisdom is a lifelong journey, a winding road filled with wonderful discoveries. Embrace every experience, for each moment holds the potential for growth and learning. Reflect on your experiences, seek knowledge from others, and remain open to the wisdom life has to offer. As we weave wisdom into our lives, we empower ourselves and those around us, creating a warm ripple effect of understanding and compassion.

In conclusion, wisdom emerges when we learn from every experience. By welcoming worthwhile challenges, seeking guidance from wise mentors, journaling our reflections, and embracing collaboration, we cultivate a wealth of insights that enrich our lives. So, let's walk the path of wisdom, weaving our experiences into a tapestry of understanding and growth.

X

Xcellence
Xceeding in Every Xperience

Xcellence is the x-factor that xceeds the ordinary. It's the xtra step you take in every xperience, the xactness in your actions, and the xploration of possibilities beyond the obvious. To xcel is not just to succeed; it's to set a new xample, one that inspires and challenges others to do the same. Think of xcellence as a constant pursuit, a path where every xecution matters and every effort adds value to the journey.

In this quest for xcellence, every xample you set has the power to shape outcomes. Like an xplorer venturing into uncharted territory, those who chase xcellence must be prepared to xamine the unknown. Xcellence doesn't come from remaining in the xpected; it emerges when you xplore the unseen, when you dare to xperiment with the unexpected.

In sports, for example, athletes don't just train to meet the standard. They push to xceed it, reaching for records previously thought unreachable. Their drive for xcellence is what separates the xtraordinary from the ordinary. Whether it's the xquisite precision of a gymnast on the balance beam or the xplosive speed of a sprinter on the track, xcellence is the force behind their success.

But xcellence is not just about athletic feats. It's present in every field. Take an artist, for instance. A painter's xcellence lies in their xpressive strokes, in their ability to bring a canvas to life. They do not settle for the first draft; they refine, they xamine, and they xperiment until the painting xceeds their initial vision. This pursuit of xcellence is what transforms an ordinary piece of art into a masterpiece.

Xcellence, like a finely tuned machine, requires xactitude in its execution. It's about fine-tuning every detail to ensure that nothing is left to chance. Imagine a watchmaker crafting an xquisite timepiece. Every gear, every screw must be placed with xact precision for the clock to function perfectly. One minor error can disrupt the entire mechanism, and this xemplifies the importance of attention to detail in the pursuit of xcellence.

In business, xcellence is often the difference between success and failure. Companies that xcel in customer service, product quality, and innovation are the ones that thrive. They don't just meet expectations; they xceed them. They understand that in a competitive world, only the xceptional survive. They invest time in xamining every aspect of their business, from employee training to product design, to ensure that every facet xudes xcellence.

Xcellence also applies to personal growth. To truly xcel, one must xamine their strengths and weaknesses with honesty. It's about being willing to improve, to xperiment with new approaches, and to xtract lessons from failure. The road to xcellence is not without setbacks, but those who xcel understand that failure is part of the process. It's an xperience that allows for growth and xploration.

In education, for example, xcellence is seen in students who not only meet the standard but xceed it by constantly xploring new ideas, asking questions, and xhibiting a thirst for knowledge. These students are the ones who go on to set new standards in their respective fields, as their pursuit of xcellence drives them to xcel beyond what's expected.

Ultimately, xcellence is about xpectation, xecution, and xploration. It's about striving for the best in every situation, leaving no stone unturned in the quest for perfection. Whether in art, sports, business, or personal growth, xcellence is the key to unlocking one's true potential.

Y

Yearning

Yielding To The Yonder You Yearn For

Yearning is the youthful yet wise yearning within you, a yearning that yanks at your very soul, whispering "Yes, you can." It's the yearning that you carry in your heart, yearning for something beyond the yardstick of your current reality. You yearn for the yonder, the unknown yet desirable, the "yet-to-come." Yearning is like a young river that yields to its path yet rushes forward to meet the ocean. You know the destination is there, but the journey, with all its ups and downs, makes the yearning even more valuable.

When you yield to your deepest yearnings, it's like wrapping yourself in a warm yet wild yoke. You feel this tension—caught between the yearning for more and the satisfaction of where you stand now. Yearning is both a yearning for change and a yearning for the comfort of the familiar. It's like the oxymoron of youth yearning for wisdom and the wise yearning for the energy of youth. You yield, yet you move forward, trusting that each step will take you closer to that "yes" moment you're yearning for.

In the everyday hustle, your yearning works as your silent yet significant guide. You yield not in weakness but in a yearning-driven pursuit of something beyond your current state. It's the yearning that allows you to say, "Yes, I'll try again" when things go awry. It's the quiet, yet powerful, "you" that refuses to say "yet" to giving up. Personified, yearning is like a young seed, always pushing toward the light, yearning for growth, no matter how much soil weighs it down.

You yearn for success, but even in that yearning, you might feel a pull toward the simpler "yesterdays"—a yearning to hold onto what's familiar. Yet, the idiom "yesterday's gone" serves as a reminder that your yearning is about the future, not the past. You yearn to go beyond the now, to explore what lies beyond the horizon. Your heart leaps for the yonder, where everything you've dreamed of awaits you.

Your yearning isn't passive; it's like a yoke that keeps you yoked to your dreams. You may feel weighed down, but the yearning doesn't let you quit. It keeps you moving toward that future you've yet to reach. This quiet, inner drive is the fuel that keeps your fire alive, even when you feel like the world is saying "no" to your dreams. Yearning's "yes" will always push you, no matter how far you've yet to go.

Like a yawn that never ends, yearning stretches out into the farthest corners of your life, reminding you that there is always more to discover, more to chase, and more to learn. Your yearning might start as a whisper, but it grows louder with every step. It's the force that keeps you saying “yes” when you’re tempted to settle for “good enough.”

The youthfulness of your yearning gives you energy, but the wisdom of it reminds you that patience is part of the process. You can’t rush the unfolding of your dreams, but you can keep yearning, moving toward that goal with every "yet" conquered. Yielding to your yearning is not weakness but a sign of your inner strength, your faith in the possibility of more.

Yearning may feel like a constant "yes" to the unknown, but that's where its power lies. It doesn’t let you rest. Instead, it whispers of what’s possible, of what’s waiting for you in the yonder you’ve yet to see. And so, you yearn, not just for the outcome but for the very journey that will take you there. Yielding to your yearning means saying “yes” to every opportunity, every challenge, and every unknown yet worth pursuing.

Z

Zeal

Zipping Through Life With Zest And Zing

Zeal is like the zesty zing of a fresh breeze, infusing your life with energy and enthusiasm. When you live with zeal, every day feels like it's buzzing with potential, as though the world is waiting to hand you opportunities wrapped in gold. The zest for life zips through your veins like a lightning bolt, charging you up to tackle tasks with zest and zoom. Zeal is what makes the seemingly impossible feel achievable. It's the zing in your step, the fire in your soul, pushing you toward what you want with a relentless drive.

With zeal, you attack your goals with a zest that never fades. You don't just meander through life, you move with the energy of a racehorse at the starting line, waiting to zoom toward the finish. It's as if every day is a new opportunity to chase the horizon, where the sun never sets on your ambition. Zeal allows you to zigzag through challenges, swiftly moving past obstacles, and keeping your focus zeroed in on the prize. You aren't deterred by zigzags in the path, but rather, you zoom through them with excitement.

Zeal is a zillion times more powerful than mere motivation. While motivation may waver, zeal is a permanent companion that never fizzles out. It's the zealot's passion for the craft, the zookeeper's careful tending to animals with enthusiasm, and the zeal that keeps a musician practicing the same piece until it's perfected. Zeal is that unwavering zest for excellence, the constant yearning to push yourself beyond the limits others see for you. It's the zero-tolerance attitude for mediocrity, demanding you give your all in everything you do.

Just like a zebra stands out in a herd, zeal sets you apart from the crowd. It's the quality that makes you zoom past others who lack the same zest for life. It's the x-factor, the secret sauce that ensures you don't blend in but blaze a trail. With zeal, you don't just walk through life—you sprint, leap, and fly through it. You bring an energy that's magnetic, drawing people toward you because they can feel the zeal radiating from you like the midday sun in the desert.

Zeal is not just excitement; it's a combination of determination and a zestful spirit. It's like a wildfire that refuses to be contained, spreading across every area of your life. You zealously guard your dreams, refusing to let anyone or anything dampen your flame. Zeal personifies your inner drive, a beacon that lights up the darkest nights, guiding you forward with an undying enthusiasm that says, "I will achieve this."

Figuratively speaking, zeal is the fuel that keeps your life's engine running at full throttle. When others are running on empty, you're zooming ahead, full of vigor and vitality. Zeal doesn't let you slow down; it demands that you keep moving, keep striving, and keep living with passion. It's what makes every mundane task feel like an exciting challenge. You approach life with a zestful curiosity, wanting to squeeze every last drop of joy and success from each moment.

Zeal is a zealot's tool, the energy that keeps you zeroed in on your goals. It's what makes you wake up early with excitement and stay up late chasing your dreams. Whether you're facing zigzagging paths or clear roads, zeal is what keeps you zooming forward. When you live with zeal, you carry an unshakable belief that your energy and enthusiasm will turn even the most difficult situations into moments of growth. Zeal ensures that you don't just exist, but that you live fully, exuberantly, and with a zest that leaves others in awe.

In the grand scheme of life, zeal is your ultimate ally. It's the zip in your step, the zest in your spirit, and the zing that brings excitement to every endeavour. Zeal transforms ordinary moments into extraordinary opportunities, allowing you to maximise your potential in every situation. Like a zooming comet in the night sky, zeal leaves a trail behind you that others will want to follow. So, hold onto your zeal, let it fuel your every move, and live life with all the zest and energy it deserves.

All adventures begin with ambition, a spark that ignites action. Boldness drives you forward, carving out opportunities where challenges may arise. Courage is the cornerstone, the fuel that helps you defy doubt and face difficulty head-on. Dreams demand dedication—each step forward, no matter how small, is part of the journey toward fulfilment.

Every endeavour requires effort, evolving through experiences and embracing failure as a friend, not a foe. Growth comes when you grasp the lessons from hardship, honing your inner strength. Hope is the hidden force, illuminating your path even when darkness clouds the horizon.

Inspiration ignites within, like a flame that refuses to fade, reminding you that limits are illusions. Joy isn't just found in the destination but in the journey—where every struggle shapes your story. Keep kindness at the forefront, for it attracts allies, making the journey lighter.

Learn to leap beyond limitations, moulding yourself through resilience and tenacity. Understand that victory isn't always immediate—it unfolds gradually as you work tirelessly. Zealously pursue your vision, knowing that the alphabet of success stretches from A to Z, with each letter playing its part in the ultimate triumph.

Your path, though winding, is yours to write—crafted with purpose, passion, and persistenc